GAP STANDERS

INTERCESSION
the weapon of choice

Brenda Todd

Gap Standers
Intercession: The Weapon of Choice
Copyright (c) 1997
Brenda J. Todd
P. O. Box 702063 | Tulsa, OK 74170

ISBN 978-1482351767

Printed in the United States of America

Library of Congress — Cataloged in Publication Data

Unless otherwise indicated, all Scripture quotations are taken from The King James Version of the Bible.

All Scripture quotations marked NIV are taken from The Holy Bible: New International Version.
Copyright (c) 1973, 1978, 1984 by The International Bible Society.
Used by permission of Zondervan Bible Publishers.

Scripture quotations marked AMP are taken from The Amplified Bible, New Testament, copyright (c) 1958, 1987 by The Lockman Foundation, La Habra, California, or The Amplified Bible, Old Testament, copyright (c) 1964, 1987 by Zondervan Publishing House, Grand Rapids, Michigan.

Printed in the United States of America. All rights reserved under International Copyright Law. Contents and/or cover may not be reproduced in whole or in part in any form without the express written consent of the Publisher.

Dedication

To My Oldest
And Much Loved Son
Gabriel Zarmesian Todd
Whose name means man of God, skilled in mediating.
I can see the attributes of a gap stander in you.

Love Mom

Acknowledgments

To my heavenly Father, who has directed me in every step of this endeavor.

To my life partner, Tomm and our four sons, Gabriel, Michael, Rapheal, and Brentom for your love, patience and understanding while spending many hours away from you during the final stages of this manuscript.

To my god-daughter, Charmaine T. Cruise who started the ball rolling by transcribing the original tapes, proof reading, making changes and e-mailing the manuscript for me. Thank you so much.

To Marilyn Price who brought form to the manuscript.

To Sylvia Earls, who God used at a very strategic time to draw out of me valuable information that was vital to the completion of this book.

To Holly Higgins, who God used to connect us to the final editor, Tom Fay, all the way in Spain, who did a great job. Thank you both.

To Destiny Marketing Group, Vince and Cindy Flores, and Chiqui Polo, for their technical assistance in cover design, final layout, and printing of this book.

To Bishop Gary McIntosh, who commanded me to write this book. Thank you To Bishop Carlton and Gina Pearson and the Higher Dimensions Family Church, the place God used for me to learn much of what I shared with you in this book.

To all the Body of Christ, especially my personal intercessors and those who have said "yes" to a lifestyle of intercession.

Foreword

I have known Brenda Todd for over 20 years now, having met her while conducting a revival in 1978 at Grambling State University in Louisiana, when she was "Miss Grambling." She had the anointing, intensity and passion for God even then. I told one of the ladies on my crusade team, "She is a natural born leader and will someday become a powerful instrument for God." Before long, she and her husband, Tommy, began traveling with my crusade team. She, singing with our praise and worship team and he, running our sound system. They have been with me ever since. They were there when we began Higher Dimensions Evangelistic Center in a small storefront building in Jenks, Oklahoma. Having grown from 75 people that first Sunday morning in 1981, to more than 5,000 people today. Brenda has been a faithful Elder in our church throughout its every phase. Today they travel this nation and the world as a powerful husband and wife team.

One integral part that Brenda plays in our ministry is that of an intercessor. This remarkably anointed lady truly knows how to pray and has for the 20 years! The powerful message she shares in her book, Gap Standers, are not intangible scriptures, but in Brenda, "the word has become flesh." She is a living example of someone who truly lives what she preaches and preaches what she lives. She is someone I would consider an "authority" on the subject of intercession, and often misunderstood and little-utilized function within the Church.

The Greek word for intercession is enteuxis and essentially means "seeking the presence and hearing of god on behalf of others." I rephrase it with a subtle play on words: "inner session." The intercessor goes into the inner sanctums of God (literally behind the veil), in the presence of god, where they experience special and deep interaction with God by the Spirit and become part and parcel of a divinely orchestrated network of battles and embattlements in the heavenlies. Intercession involves a powerful utterance in both the soulish and spirit realm.

The intercessor, through both his prayer and thought life, makes himself or herself a vehicle through which the Divine gains tangible access to the temporal and activates the will of God in the earthly domains. Intercessors are Holy Spirit possessed in the same manner derelicts are possessed by demons.

Intercession at its zenith causes intervention, sometimes even by angels, as was the case in the New Testament narrative relating Peter's life-threatening imprisonment and subsequent deliverance through angelic assistance, commanded into this realm through the effectual fervent prayers of the saints (Acts 12:5-18).

When Brenda is flowing in her powerful ministry calling, she becomes a Holy Spirit possessed person, and through her, God intervenes to interrupt the normal, natural process of the temporal present, and substitutes it with a heavenly flow of infinite actions and transactions that can change lives and conditions forever.

This book will teach you how to access and activate that same power and pass it on. I encourage you to not just read Gap Standers, but to study it, devour it. It is certain to become one of the most important books in your library.

Bishop Carlton D. Pearson
Senior Pastor, Higher Dimensions Family Church
Presiding Bishop, Azusa Interdenominational Fellowship
Tulsa, Oklahoma

Table of Contents

Foreword

Introduction

1. Who is Called to be An Intercessor? 19

2. Sitting at Jesus' Feet 29

3. Going Through "God's Process" 39

4. Possessing a Servant's Attitude 51

5. Strengthening Your Foundation 55

6. Praying the Word 61

7. Persistence in Prayer 67

8. Flowing With the Vision of the House   71

9. Overcoming Discouragement   77

10. Your "Shunammite Blessing" Is in the House   81

11. Changing "Barren" Circumstances Through Intercession   85

12. Jesus -- The Greatest Intercessor   99

I sought a man among them who should build up the wall and stand in the gap before Me for the land, that I should not destroy it, but I found none.

Ezekiel 22:30 (AMP)

Therefore, my beloved brethren, be firm (steadfast), immovable, always abounding in the work of the Lord [always being superior, excelling, doing more than enough in the service of the Lord], knowing and being continually aware that your labor in the Lord is not futile [it is never wasted or to no purpose].

1 Corinthians 15:58 (AMP)

Introduction

My husband and I have been with Higher Dimensions Family Church in Tulsa, Oklahoma, under the pastorate of Bishop Carlton Pearson, for more than sixteen years. While in college in Louisiana at Grambling State University, I met my husband, Tommy. We attended a revival that Pastor Carlton held at the college and have been involved with his ministry ever since.

I grew up knowing little about prayer and even less about praise and worship. I could barely pray for five minutes! But now God has called me to stand alongside leadership to give aid, advice and counsel in the areas of praise and worship, and intercession.

Although I will touch briefly on the area of praise and worship in this book, my primary emphasis will be on the topic of intercession. I talk about praise and worship and intercession together because they are two wings of the same bird. If you get your praise and worship and intercession right, then you will go somewhere — both individually and as a church family.

The flow of the praise and worship and intercession will either enhance or destroy what the spiritual leadership tries to do. This is why it is so important to be in tune with the Holy Spirit. You must learn to pray specifically — to aim for the bull's-eye in prayer.

My goal is to clarify some of the misconceptions regarding **intercession** and **intercessors**, and to challenge you today to embrace the call to **"Stand in the Gap"** (1 Tim.2:1-4). Become a **Gap Stander!** My prayer is that you will be better equipped to do so after having read this book.

Who Is Called to Be An Intercessor?

Who is called to be an Intercessor? You Are! We Are!

Intercession is one of the most misunderstood areas in the Church. Its purpose and power have been diminished through tradition and ignorance.

Every Christian is called to be an intercessor. Let's dispel some of the misconceptions of who intercessors are and what intercession entails, and consider the importance of intercession in bringing God's purposes into manifestation in the earth.

Intercession does not refer to your personal communication with God on your own behalf. Intercession is another level in prayer. It means "<u>to stand in the gap in prayer in behalf of someone else</u>." 1 It is the willingness to be a link between God and man.

First of all, then, I admonish and urge that petitions, prayers, intercessions, and thanksgivings be offered on behalf of <u>all men</u>.

For kings and all who are in positions of authority or high responsibility, that [outwardly] we may pass a quiet and undisturbed life [and inwardly] a peaceable one in all godliness and reverence and seriousness in every way.

For such [praying] is good and right, and [it is] pleasing and acceptable to God our Savior,

Who wishes all men to be saved and [increasingly] to perceive and recognize and discern and know precisely and correctly the [divine] Truth.

1 Timothy 2:1-4 (AMP)

---

1 Miriam Webster Dictionary INC., (Springdale, Massachusetts, U.S.A., 1983).

In many churches and ministries, prayer has been relegated to a few chosen people. However, we see in these verses that Paul was addressing the Church both individually and corporately regarding their responsibility to intercede. Paul encouraged the people of God as a Body to intercede. Intercession was not a "ministry" (as many today believe it to be). It was encouraged and taught as a <u>lifestyle</u> to be embraced and developed by everyone.

A misconception that has infiltrated the Church for many decades, one that must be destroyed, is that intercession is only done by a few people, usually women, who are spiritually unbalanced or "off." These people are portrayed as having a lot of idle time on their hands. They sit in a poorly lit room moaning and groaning for hours, yelling and screaming as if they were mad at the devil <u>and</u> at God.

This belief, held by many, is far from the truth. Even though God said in Jeremiah 9:17 to call for the "wailing women," women who are skilled in prayer, there is a call on <u>every</u> child of God to join his or her elder brother, Jesus Christ, in daily intercession.

We are to imitate Christ in every aspect of our lives. He was and is a Man given over to intercession. He did nothing without first laboring in intercession before God the Father. He understood the importance of communing with the Father to obtain strength and instruction before going to the multitudes. Even now, Jesus Christ makes intercession on behalf of all the saints. He is the Chief Intercessor.

It is Christ that died, yea rather, that is risen again, who is even at the right hand of God, who also maketh intercession for us.

Romans 8:34

In my travels in the United States and other countries, I have found the intercessory prayer base in many churches, both large and small, to be very weak or nonexistent. As a result, many churches and ministries are ineffective in carrying out their God-ordained purpose in the earth. Although some might appear to be prospering, the vision of God (the initial intent of God for that house or ministry) remains obstructed or dormant. Intercessors have either vacated their posts or have not answered the call.

Just as blood is a vital entity to the existence of the natural body, intercession is vital to the body of Christ. Loss of intercession, like loss of blood, will cause sickness or weakness, or, in some instances, death. We have within us the ability to bring healing to the Body of Christ and to our land through intercession.

If My people, who are called by My name, shall humble themselves, pray, seek, crave, and require of necessity My face and turn from their wicked ways, then will I hear from heaven, forgive their sin, and heal their land.

Now My eyes will be open and My ears attentive to prayer offered in this place.

2 Chronicles 7:14, 15 (AMP)

God has obligated Himself to hear the intercessions of His people, to answer and produce on their behalf.

Although it was prophesied several times in the Old Testament that Jesus Christ the Messiah would come to save the world from sin, people such as Anna and Simeon still labored in intercession for years until Jesus was manifested in the flesh. This is the kind of intercession which pleases God and affects change in the natural.

What many Christians fail to understand is that there is constant warfare going on in heavenly places against the perfect plan, will and purpose of God. Too many people in the body of Christ are spiritually dressed in wedding clothes anticipating the coming of the Lord. But this is a time of war: we must be dressed in army fatigues and combat boots ready for warfare.

The Bible instructs us to put on the whole armor of God that we may be able to stand against the wiles (deception, craftiness and cunning) of the devil (Eph. 6:13). If God's people are dressed inappropriately for battle, they will not be protected from the enemy's darts. But as believers take their positions in the gap as intercessors, not wavering but persevering, the purposes of God will manifest successfully in the earth. The lives and hearts of people will be eternally transformed.

How Do We Take Our Place as Intercessors?

Ultimately, it is the Holy Spirit Who teaches us how to intercede.

> *Likewise the Spirit also helpeth our infirmities: for we know not what we should pray for as we ought: but the Spirit itself maketh intercession for us with groanings which cannot be uttered.*
>
> *And he that searcheth the hearts knoweth what is the mind of the Spirit, because he*

maketh intercession for the saints according to the will of God.

Romans 8:26, 27

The following five elements are essential for laying a good foundation in the area of intercession:

1. Develop a personal relationship and prayer life with God. This will determine the depth to which you can intercede on behalf of others.

2. Examine the condition of your heart. God stated that we are to seek Him with all our heart (Jer. 29:13). Many come before God with hearts divided. Things such as anger, lust, idols, bitterness, unforgiveness and pride handicap effectual intercession and hinder the manifestation of answers to prayer.

3. Pray according to the Word of God. It is imperative to find Scripture that pertains to the subject you are interceding about. God's Word will not return void, but will accomplish what it was sent out to do (Isaiah 55:11). Praying God's Word prevents us from praying ineffective, soulish or manipulative prayers.

4. Pray in faith believing. Intercession must be continually sharpened by faith, one of the cornerstones upon which a Christian's life is built. *Without faith it is impossible to please him [God]: for he that cometh to God must believe that he is, and that he is a rewarder of them that diligently seek him.*

Hebrews 11:6

5. Persevere in intercession. Don't give up regardless of what the situation looks like in the natural.

Many of God's people do not consider themselves qualified to be intercessors due to struggles encountered in their personal lives of prayer. But intercession is birthed out of God's love (See 1 Corinthians 13:1-13). God commands us to love one another. We do not consider our own interests but the interests and needs of others.

> *Therefore if there is any consolation in Christ, if any comfort of love, if any fellowship of the Spirit, if any affection and mercy,*
>
> *fulfill my joy by being like-minded, having the same love, being of one accord, of one mind.*

Let nothing be done through selfish ambition or conceit, but in lowliness of mind let each esteem others better than himself.

Let each of you look out not only for his own interests, but also for the interests of others.

Let this mind be in you which was also in Christ Jesus.

Philippians 2:1-5 (NKJV)

The Bible also states, **Greater love hath no man than this, that a man lay down his life for his friends** (John 15:13). As intercessors, we momentarily lay our own needs aside in order to petition God on behalf of others. As we remain faithful to stand in the gap in prayer for others, God will not forget our labor of love and will meet our needs as well.

Praying always with all prayer and supplication in the Spirit, and watching thereunto with all perseverance and supplication for all saints.
Ephesians 6:18

Through intercession, we cover one another — our leaders, families and ministries — with the shed blood of Jesus Christ This blood contains all the elements for protection, prosperity, health and well-being in every area of life.

It is time for the entire body of Christ to get a different perspective, a godly view as it were, of the importance of intercession and its place in the life of believers. Be strengthened as you gain a clearer understanding of <u>your role</u> in intercession— in Jesus' name.

Sitting at Jesus' Feet

God needs people who will intercede. He needs you. If you are going to be a **Gap Stander** — one who prays in behalf of others — you must have a relationship with God through a personal life of prayer.

I have found that not enough of us spend personal time before the Lord. Yet it is in prayer and in spending time in His Word that we get to know Him.

The Bible says there will be those who come before Him to whom He will say, **I never knew you: depart from me, ye that work iniquity** (Mat. 7:23). The word <u>knew</u> here means: "to be intimately acquainted with or familiar with; to discern, come to know; to recognize as the nature of; to have a practical understanding of."[2] Jesus is saying, "There was never a time when we were alone, a time when we were intimate, a time when I could talk with you or when you sat in My presence.

---

[2] W. E. Vine, Expository Dictionary of Biblical Words (Nashville: Thomas Nelson Publishers, 1985), p. 298.

You say, "But Lord, I prophesied in Your name." Jesus' response is, "But you didn't <u>know</u> Me."

Again you say, "Lord, I cast out devils in Your name." He responds again, "But you didn't <u>know</u> Me."

Many of us get so caught up in the <u>work of the Lord</u> that we don't get caught up in the <u>LORD of the work.</u> There must be time for the building of a relationship with Jesus. We should do everything in relationship with Him.

It takes time in His presence to develop a relationship with Jesus. Some people say, "I don't have time." We don't have time <u>not</u> to be with Him if we are going to be effective in what He has called us to do.

Christians, we've got to wake up! We have to ask God to give us ears to hear what the Spirit of the Lord is saying. Jesus, our perfect example, often went into places of solitude to seek the Lord. Jesus never went about His day acting independently of His Father. He remained in the presence of God until He received instructions and solutions. Jesus was confident in Who He was and what He was instructed to do because He was in relationship and communication with the One that had sent Him.
The Lord God has given Me the tongue of the learned, that I should know how to speak a word in season to him who is weary. He awakens Me

morning by morning, He awakens My ear to hear as the learned. The Lord God has opened My ear, and I was not rebellious, nor did I turn away. Isaiah 50:4-5 (NKJV)

It is imperative that we get before God and obtain our directives from Him morning by morning. If the Lord wakes you up at 3:00 am, do not rebel or turn away. We toil and labor over decisions and difficulties that God desires to resolve before we step out of the door. But, first, we must get before Him.

In Luke 10:38-42 (NIV), look at the differing reactions of Mary and Martha to a visit Jesus made to their home:

> As Jesus and his disciples were on their way, he came to a village where a woman named Martha opened her home to him.
>
> She had a sister called Mary, who sat at the Lord's feet listening to what he said.
>
> But Martha was distracted by all the preparations that had to be made. She came to him and asked, "Lord, don't you care that my sister has left me to do the work by myself?
>
> Tell her to help me!"

"Martha, Martha," the Lord answered, "you are worried and upset about many things, but only one thing is needed. Mary has chosen what is better, and it will not be taken away from her."

We are talking about the development of an intimate relationship with Jesus. While Mary sat at Jesus' feet obtaining wisdom and knowledge, Martha was distracted, worried and upset about all the preparations. You can get so harassed by the things that you are involved in, the business of life, that you don't have time to talk or listen to Jesus, the giver of life.

I've heard God speak to me at different times of my life, "Brenda, stop 'Martha-ing'!" These were times when I was consumed with life's challenges and circumstances. Mary found the "needful" thing to do: to sit at Jesus' feet. If we are going to be effective for God, we must find the time for the "needful" part: getting to know Jesus by coming into His presence and staying awhile! You will be able to accomplish everything you need to do when He is given His place.

In sitting at Jesus' feet, Jesus taught Mary how to deal with offenses and life's challenges. She found out how to deal with circumstances God's way. Most Christians try to handle too many problems and situations in their flesh without Jesus' help, guidance and direction.

When we come to God's feet, He takes us to a higher level and allows us to see things from His perspective. From His viewpoint, we can look down and see things the way they really are.

Your view of a city from an airplane is different than when you are on the ground. From the plane you can see the entire city; from the ground you see only a small area. Often, what looks big on the ground looks like a molehill from God's perspective. God will not only answer us when we call upon Him, but He will also reveal those things that were hidden from us previously. The Lord will give His people revelational insight and strategy during those times of <u>intimacy</u> with Him. God wants the righteous to rise up and be Gap Standers for families, for the lost, for the church, and for nations.

The lower we sit at Jesus' feet, the higher He will lift us spiritually until we are in God's face. And to be effective in prayer, we have to get in God's face. There is no other way. In God's face, He will reveal His secrets.
> *Call unto me and I will answer thee, and shew thee great and mighty things, which thou knowest not.*
>
> *Jeremiah 33:3*

Strengthening Your Relationship With God

Many times we do not listen when we sit at Jesus' feet. Instead, we talk incessantly. We tell Jesus problems we see in the church, problems about our involvement in various projects, problems with and about certain people. We need to sit at Jesus' feet as Mary did and <u>listen</u> to what He has to say.

Too often we take our own agenda to the Lord. He is trying to shine light on the whole matter so we will come out on top, but, instead, we just want to discuss the little portion we see. God does not want us to be harassed or diverted by anything — including our ministry.

Mary had been at Jesus' feet before. She actually wept on His feet. But she did not stop there; she unwrapped her hair and dried His feet with her hair (Luke 7:37; John 11:2). A woman's hair is her glory. She took what was hers and wiped Jesus' feet. To me that says "servant."

This woman did not mind serving. She did not mind saying, "I humble myself under Your mighty hand, Lord, so You can do the work that needs to be done in me." When we stay in Jesus' face, it helps us to realize that we, as intercessors, are not the big deal. Jesus is!

Mary took an alabaster box of precious ointment and broke it open to anoint Jesus. The house was filled with the fragrance of the very costly oil. The sacrifice of a year's wages did not matter to Mary, because she desired to offer her best. It was a sacrifice of praise.

Are you willing to praise Him? To worship Him? To cause a sweet incense to go up to Him? That's relationship. Mary did that.

Let's not go to the feet of Jesus only when we need to get a "message." Everything that we do should be birthed out of relationship with Jesus. Mary chose the better part. The better part was at Jesus' feet.

Physically, your feet bring balance to your body, they serve as your base. Being in prayer at the feet of Jesus is your base — your foundation for ministry and for all of life itself! One of the most humbling experiences you can have is to wash someone's feet. Healing comes through foot washing. If you are having a mess in your church with people, call for a foot washing service. It brings humility and forgiveness — and both contribute to building and strengthening relationships.

Just as we have different kinds of feet, we have different types of people in the body of Christ. We have to know how to deal with all kinds of "feet."

Have you ever had shoes that fit too tight? Have you ever had somebody step on your feet?

Unfortunately, there are some people who are easily offended. It's like accidentally stepping on their feet. Sometimes you don't even know that they have been offended or stepped on. Certainly that was not the intent. But at the feet of Jesus that you will learn how to help people who take offense too easily.

Jesus said, **"It is impossible but that offences will come: but woe unto him, through whom they come"** (Luke. 17:1). Offenses will come, but it is at the feet of Jesus where likewise we learn how to deal with our own offenses.

Have you ever known someone who had a diseased foot —or maybe something as simple as athlete's foot? Just as there are natural diseases, there can be diseases of the spirit. It is at the feet of Jesus where we learn how to deal with these diseases of the spirit: jealousy, envy, strife, bitterness, etc.
It's time we learn how to undergird one another's ministries. It's time to start networking with other Christians and undergirding one another in prayer. Excellence in ministry will develop as we uphold one another in prayer.

"Relationship" is the key for developing an effective prayer life. In relationship through intercession, you will bring heaven to earth in your life, your marriage, home and family, your church, your ministry, and into the lives of those for whom you are interceding.

To be a true intercessor, you must have a relationship with the Lord. Do you have a consistent time of prayer with the Lord on a daily basis? If not, why not stop right now and pray. Ask the Holy Spirit to show you what time you should begin to meet Him daily. Make a quality decision now. Let's pray together:

Father, forgive me for not spending a <u>daily</u> time of prayer with you. I'm making a fresh commitment with my life to meet you for prayer at:_____(Put in Specific Time.)

Thank you, Lord, for meeting me at our appointed time and drawing nigh to me as I draw nigh to you. Amen.

Signed:_____

Date:_____

Going Through "God's Process"

God has a process. If we are going to be God's people, we have to be willing to go through God's process. This process includes a time of preparation.

Believers who obey God are repeatedly processed. They may not always understand the process as they go through trials and difficult circumstances, but coming out wiser and stronger.

This is the word that came to Jeremiah from the Lord: "Go down to the potter's house, and there I will give you my message." So I went down to the potter's house, and I saw him working at the wheel. But the pot he was shaping from the clay was marred in his hands; so the potter formed it into another pot, shaping it as seemed best to him.

> Then the word of the Lord came to me: "O house of Israel, can I not do with you as this potter does?" declares the Lord. "Like clay

in the hand of the potter, so are you in my hand, O house of Israel."

Jeremiah 18:1-6 (NIV)

To be effective ministers, preachers, evangelists, prophets, or children of God, we must be willing to go through His process. Likewise, to be effective intercessors for God, we must be willing to go through His process.

God gives us a vivid illustration of this process in Jeremiah 18 where we see the potter refining, reshaping and remodeling a clay vessel. The clay the potter was shaping became marred. <u>Marred</u> means "messed up; injured; hurt; damaged; spoiled."[3]

Many of us have been marred by life's circumstance. Some injuries are self-inflicted while others result from the actions of others. It doesn't matter how you were hurt or damaged. God wants to shape you into what He originally had in mind.

In the initial process of restoration, God begins to dig us out of sin, a place of desolation. He redeems our lives from death.

---

3 Miriam Webster Dictionary INC., (Springdale, Massachusetts, U.S.A., 1985).

But the process doesn't stop there. Next, intense shaping begins. Renewing and remaking of our minds take place as we stop conforming to the world. We start to establish and develop relationship with God through a personal life of prayer, and by reading and studying God's Word. Through consistency and sound teaching we begin to develop as effective intercessors.

Then God starts working on us to teach us how to commune with Him, how to hear and petition Him for others as well as for ourselves.

Years ago, if I prayed for fifteen minutes, I thought I was accomplishing a great feat in the spirit realm. I prayed "for me, my four and no more!" But God began His "process" on me and helped me to realize there were depths in prayer and intercession that were not charted by me. I had not even gone beneath the surface.

God sent three special women to me who made a significant difference in my prayer life. Carol Garver, one of those special women, taught me accountability in prayer. She prayed with me on a daily basis for two hours a day for almost a year. (We probably prayed together some 500 hours!)

Carol helped me to establish prayer as a priority. At that time in my life, I had two young babies who demanded a lot of care and attention. However, I was taught to schedule prayer in my daily routine, and to schedule out phone calls and other distractions.

Another special woman, Astrid Barron, became a mother of Zion to me with special regard for prayer. She taught me persistence and tenacity in prayer, how to pray until change came. I learned how to stand firm in the gap for many people I had never seen or known in the natural. Through prayer, they became a real part of my life.

My precious friend Pam Vinnett taught me how to labor and press even further in intercession until circumstances were altered in the spirit realm. During our 13-year friendship, she has been instrumental in teaching me prophetic intercession. I learned how to intercede based upon what God said prophetically rather than upon present situations and circumstances.

As I continued to remain in God's process, I went from praying fifteen minutes a day to three or more hours a day. As you remain in the process, God will also develop a prayer life that is suitable for you. You will last longer in prayer as you allow Him to work with, in and through you. If you are willing to go through God's process, you will become God's person, and He will transform your life.

When the clay got marred, the potter didn't throw it away. He took that same piece of clay and put it back up on that wheel and began to shape it again as it pleased him.

Any time you start shaping and working with clay to make it into something new, you can expect some resistance. The more the clay pushes back, the harder God has to push down on it to shape it. God's process doesn't always feel good because some things in our lives have to be severed, stretched or molded.

The process of being developed into an intercessor is uncomfortable. It is as if you are in a holding pattern. Nothing exciting seems to be taking place. You may feel like you are the only one laboring before the Lord. You may even wonder if all that intercession you're doing is making a difference. But that is a part of the shaping process, and you must be willing to hang in there — even if no one hangs with you!

In the Scripture passage we read earlier of Jesus' visit to Mary and Martha's house (Luke 10:38-42), Mary made a choice to go through God's process. She sat at Jesus' feet to learn of Him and commune with Him while Martha was "worried" and "upset" about natural things. Jesus said to Martha, **"But only one thing is needed. Mary has chosen what is** *better, and it will not be taken away from her"* (v. 42, NIV).

We have to make a choice daily to go through the processes that God desires to put us through, as His children and as His ministers. We may be at different levels in the process, but we have to be willing to obey God. If you want to be an intercessor, you have to be willing to do what an intercessor does — stand in the gap interceding for others and, at times, with others.

Martha was busy. Today, ministers get so busy and involved with meetings and committees and auxiliaries and visitations that they don't have time for Jesus, the Man they are supposed to be working for! They start working for a man, rather than the Man. Statistics show that ministers pray 23 minutes a day on the average. This is indicative of why the church and the world are in the shape they are today.

You can't be so involved in the business of ministry and then expect to be fresh to minister and communicate the mind of God to the people of God. It is imperative that God's leaders minister first to God, then permit Him to minister back to them before they serve God's people.

The enemy loves to keep God's people out of the place of prayer. When you wake up to pray, the devil will wake you up and get your mind racing with thoughts of obligations and scheduled appointments, tempting you to vacate your post as an intercessor.

Jesus said, "Martha, Martha . . . you are worried and upset about many things" (v. 41, NIV). Sometimes He has to call our name twice to get our attention because we are so busy. Jesus declared that Mary had found the only thing that was needful — sitting at His feet, taking time out to be in His presence.

As believers we are obligated to get in God's face on a one-on-one basis. God makes and molds us in His presence. The potter in Jeremiah 18 took the same clay. The Bible doesn't say He reached over and pulled off another piece of clay. He took the same piece of clay, put it back on the wheel, and began to reshape it as it pleased him. Transformation is dependent on how often we go before God and permit Him to process us.

God knows the call He has on each of our lives, but He wants to reconstruct us so we are prepared to step into that calling. Too many of us are trying to be cut out of the same mold as someone we hold in high esteem. But God is saying, "Be cut out of My mold." Don't permit people and circumstances to dictate to you who you are. The way you find out your individual mold is through your relationship with the Lord.

The Shelf Experience

Before the potter finishes making a clay pot, he places it on the shelf to harden. He has to make sure that during molding, the amounts of oxygen captured in the clay is reduced. If this process is omitted, the pot will burst or crack when it is placed in the fire.

So what does God do to you? He removes the things that obstruct your progress in His process. God will use circumstances and people to help get the "you" out of you. This occurs before you are placed on the shelf.

When I say you are "placed on the shelf," I am referring to the hardening or drying process that you must go through. When on the shelf, there are different things that people do. Some shout, "Hey, I'm ready, Lord. Why don't You see me? It's my turn." He says, "No, you sit on the shelf for a season."

Some people murmur and complain from the shelf. Some people shout from the shelf. Some people become jealous of others. "Why are they being exalted and I'm not?" But the "you" is getting out of you! When you get to the point when you can say, "Lord, not my will but Yours be done," God can promote you to the next level in the process.

You may think you are ready to get off the shelf. But God wants to help you go through the complete process. Stay in relationship with Him. Don't fuss about where God puts you. He is building you up for His purpose. God is laying a foundation in you.

In 1988, I went to London, England, with sixteen other people to preach, witness and lead praise and worship. Before I went, God gave me a little glimpse that He had "called me to preach." (God will give you a view of what He has placed in you, also.) I was aware of this gift, but I had never stepped out in that aspect of ministry.

When I was raising money for the trip, God said to me, "Go back to your hometown in Shreveport, Louisiana and preach, and you will be blessed financially." It was true! When I obeyed, the Lord honored His word to me.

<u>After</u> my "official" taste of preaching and my trip to England, I received my shelf experience. God told me to lay down everything. I stopped doing praise and worship. I quit my husband's singing group. I stopped being an altar worker at church. It was a big struggle for me, but I laid everything down.

My friends thought I had lost my mind! People asked me, "When are you going to sing again? Why aren't you involved anymore? What's wrong?" But God needed to get the Brenda out of Brenda! There were some areas in my life that had to be further refined. He wanted to remove the impurities because He didn't want me to crack.

During this time I fasted and prayed, and went on seven-day shut-ins. It was then that God began showing me what I was really like. It was a depressing time in my life because I didn't like what I saw. Every day I would pray the prayer of repentance. Everything in me that could be shaken was shaken. God was dealing with me. This was His process and my shelf experience. Everybody else was shouting at me and trying to get me off the shelf, but I said, "O God, do in me what You need to do." I was on that shelf for two and a half years!

I didn't know it would take that long. Before then I thought I was one of God's most obedient servants in the whole wide world. During those times of intimacy with God, He was able to deal with me about areas of my life that were not pleasing to Him.

When you get into God's face, He will get in your face. He will start putting His finger on areas in your life that are not pleasing to Him. If you will submit yourself under the mighty hand of God, like clay yielding to a potter, you will become a vessel fit for the Master's use.

If you want to become the person God has called you to be, expect some shelf experiences.

Let's pray this prayer:

Lord, I yield my life to you. Show me areas in my life that are not pleasing to you. Help me to change. I want to be what You have predestined me to be. I leave my life in your hands. Amen.

Possessing a Servant's Attitude

God places people in certain regions, in certain leadership positions, for a purpose He has in mind. As you support the vision of the church where God places you, He will cause your own vision to mature and manifest. You won't be a renegade. Renegade means "a deserter from one faith, cause or allegiance to another."[4]

There are too many people without accountability or allegiance. They become a law unto themselves. They do not have a heart of servitude. One of the results of this lack of accountability and allegiance is that the body of Christ suffers a lack of true growth. Instead of growth, there are a lot of "transplants," people going from church to church without ever getting involved.

---

[4] Miriam Webster Dictionary INC., (Springdale, Massachusetts, U.S.A., 1983).

When my husband and I hooked up with Higher Dimensions, we had our own vision. But we were also willing to submit to the leadership and vision of the church. We knew that God would not allow the vision He had placed in us to die. God will place you with people who will help draw out what He has placed in you.

Because we were willing to submit, we did a little of everything. We helped with the children. We did secretarial work. We cleaned toilets. We helped run the sound system. We became involved with prayer and intercession. You name it, and we did it. In other words, we had a servant's attitude. But that doesn't mean being willing to have the heart of a servant and being willing to serve others is easy.

We have an enemy who does not want any ministry to accomplish what God has in mind. Therefore, in order to defeat the enemy and accomplish God's purposes, God needs intercessors with the hearts of servants.

Philippians 2:7 says that Jesus **made himself of no reputation, and took upon him the form of a servant, and was made in the likeness of men.** We are to be like Jesus.

> And whosoever will be chief among you, let him be your servant:

Even as the Son of man came not to be ministered unto, but to minister, and to give his life a ransom for many.
Matthew 20:27, 28

Are you willing to be a servant? Many times we want to be lifted up in the eyes of men without first being a servant to others. It doesn't work that way! First develop a servant's attitude — with Jesus and with other believers. Only then can you develop fully as an intercessor.

Strengthening Your Foundation

Several years ago I began to help facilitate intercessory prayer for our church. At that time many doors were opening for the ministry of the church, but there were also many adversaries. It seemed that on every new level there was a new devil! Effective intercessory prayer was essential to carry forth the church vision, to take advantage of the opportunities which were before us.

God has given us prayer as one of the mighty weapons from His arsenal to ensure that His will goes forth unhindered.

Often in prayer meetings, there is confusion. One person is in a corner hollering, someone else is in another corner crying, and another is speaking loudly in tongues. People may come with their own prayer needs or with their own agendas, crying out about their own needs, when, in fact, they could have prayed about their own needs at home. True intercession, on the contrary, <u>is standing in the gap in prayer in behalf of others.</u>

As you stand in the gap for another person or for the church, God will take care of your needs and move on your behalf. Many people are so caught up with their own problems that they must be taught to reach beyond themselves.

The intercessory prayer leader must be strong in the areas of personal prayer and meditation on God's Word. In addition, the intercessory prayer leader, as well as the praise and worship leader, must have a strong prophetic ear. A person with a prophetic ear is one who is in tune with God, speaking and praying forth the will and purposes of God for that time and season.

We need sensitive prayer leaders. This sensitivity comes through relationship with God and others.

The saints are in war, so intercessors need a wartime mentality. They must be alert to the fact that it is the enemy's aim to sabotage everything God wants to do for us, in us, and through us. Each of us needs to take our place in the war.

A good description of leaders and intercessors working together is found in Exodus 17:11-13:

And it came to pass, when Moses held up his hand, that Israel prevailed: and when he let down his hand, Amalek prevailed.

But Moses' hands were heavy; and they took a stone, and put it under him, and he sat thereon; and Aaron and Hur stayed up his hands, the one on the one side, and the other on the other side; and his hands were steady until the going down of the sun.

And Joshua discomfited Amalek and his people with the edge of the sword.

This is a prime example of the "intercessors," Aaron and Hur, holding up the heavy hands of the "pastor," Moses. That is the job intercessors do. They hold up the hands of the leader and relieve the pressure of the battle which previously was directly on leader alone.

As a result, Joshua, another member of this ministry team, received tremendous power to WIN! This is **Standing in the Gap**.

When I see the enemy trying to sabotage a service at our church, the Spirit of God quickens me immediately to come against whatever forces of darkness are trying to manifest. I rise up to overcome and overthrow. This is an example of "holding up my pastor's hands." This sensitivity is developed from a strong foundation of prayer.

Praise Will Break Satan's Hold

In Acts, chapter 16, Paul and Silas were in jail for casting a demon out of a young, fortune-telling girl.

> *The crowd joined in the attack against Paul and Silas, and the magistrates ordered them to be stripped and beaten. After they had been severely flogged, they were thrown into prison, and the jailer was commanded to guard them carefully. Upon receiving such orders, he put them in the inner cell and fastened their feet in the stocks.*
>
> *About midnight Paul and Silas were praying and singing hymns to God, and the other prisoners were listening to them. Suddenly there was such a violent earthquake that the foundations of the prison were shaken. At once all the prison doors flew open, and everybody's chains came loose. The jailer woke up, and when he saw the prison doors open, he drew his sword and was about to kill himself because he thought the prisoners had escaped. But Paul shouted,*
>
> *Don't harm yourself! We are all here! The jailer called for lights.*

Acts 16:22-29 (NIV)

If intercession and praise and worship are right, a loosing or an untying of the chains and bonds that grip the people will take place. Many people who come to church need to be loosed. They need to be untied.

God has given us a commission to loose people from the works of the devil. He told us to bring deliverance to the captives and healing. That's all part of the commission. If we get intercession and praise and worship right, people will be loosed and they will go free. There will be deliverance in the house. There will be breakthroughs in the church and in the lives of individuals. Glory to God!

As my husband and I travel in ministry in the United States and abroad, we are seeing mighty miracles, not just "headache miracles." When you start loosing God's people, you won't have to worry about the number of people coming to your church or supporting your ministry.

Get on your face and ask God for His strategies to strengthen your foundations in intercession, both for your church and for yourself.

- 6 -

Praying the Word

As a ministry or an individual moves to a new level spiritually, the intercession needs to move up to another level, also. Don't be intimidated if God wants to lift prayer to another level. Never hold onto a position as if it is yours and you own it. You must be willing to move with what God is doing and enjoy the ride!

Intercessory prayer must be focused and targeted just as a missile is aimed at a target. The intercession goes forth by the anointing, then explodes and destroys every yoke of bondage.

When you begin a session of intercession with other people, take a time of cleansing and refreshing for the first five or ten minutes. When people come into prayer they usually have all kinds of things on their mind. If you have been talking "ugly" to your husband, wife, or children, you must get it cleared up so you can go to the Lord with a clean heart and clean hands.

Who may ascend the hill of the Lord? Who may stand in his holy place? He who has clean hands and a pure heart, who does not lift up his soul to an idol or swear by what is false. He will receive blessing from the Lord and vindication from God his Savior. Such is the generation of those who seek him.

Psalm 24:3-6 (NIV)

When you begin to pray, know the "target" and aim for it. The intercessory prayer leader should call out the target to the intercessors. For example, "Let's pray for our pastor." That way, you are praying for the same thing.

You learn how to "aim" your prayers by believing and speaking the promises of God's Word. You will keep your intercessors from getting off target by praying the Word.

Sometimes we deal with situations in the spirit that must be broken up. They might be things that have been laid in the very foundation of the ministry. In those cases you need what I call a "Holy Ghost jackhammer"! We've got to go in and hammer things up so God, by His Spirit, can come in and lay the foundation the way it is supposed to be. We become Holy Ghost jackhammers. The intercessors go forth in the Holy Spirit breaking up everything that isn't of God. This allows God to come in and lay the right foundation.

If nothing seems to be moving in intercession, ask God to show you His strategies for praying. The Holy Spirit will help you intercede. He is the One called alongside to help, aid, advise and counsel you. The Holy Spirit will take hold together with you in your time of intercession. Glory to God!

Proverbs 21:1 says, **The king's heart is in the hand of the Lord ... he turneth it whithersoever he will.** As you are faithful to pray God's Word, He will change people's hearts, situations and circumstances.

There is safety in praying the Word. Here are three examples. In the blank spaces insert the names of the people for whom you are praying. You may pray these prayers over yourself as well.

From Psalm 1:1-3

Blessed is _____ who walks not in the counsel of the ungodly, nor stands in the path of sinners, nor sits in the seat of the scornful. _____'s delight is in the law of the Lord; and in His law _____ meditates day and night. _____ shall be like a tree planted by the rivers of water. _____ shall bring forth fruit in his (or her) season and his (or her) leaf shall not wither.

Whatever _____ does will prosper.

From Ephesians 1:17-23 (NIV)

I pray that the God of our Lord Jesus Christ, the glorious Father, may give you,_____ the Spirit of wisdom and revelation, so that you may know Him better. I pray also that the eyes of your heart, _____, may be enlightened so you will know the hope to which He has called you, the riches of His glorious inheritance in the saints, and His incomparably great power for you who believe. This power is like the working of His mighty strength, which He exerted in Christ when He raised Him from the dead and seated Him at His right hand in the heavenly realms, far above all rule and authority, power and dominion, and every title that can be given, not only in the present age but also in the one to come. God placed all things under His feet (and under your feet, _____, as a believer in the Lord Jesus Christ), and appointed Him to be the head over everything for the Church, which is His Body, the fullness of Him Who fills everything in every way.

From Ephesians 3:14-21 (NIV)

_____ kneels before the Father, from whom His whole family in heaven and on earth derives its name. I pray that out of His glorious riches He may strengthen you, _____, with power through His Spirit in your inner being, so that Christ may dwell in your heart through faith. And I pray that you, _____, being rooted and established in love, may have power, together with all the saints, to grasp how wide and long and high and deep is the love of Christ, and to know this love that surpasses knowledge — that you, _____, may be filled to the measure of all the fullness of God.

Now, to Him who is able to do immeasurably more than all we ask or imagine, according to His power that is at work within you, _____, to Him be glory in the Church and in Christ Jesus throughout all generations, forever and ever! Amen.

Praying the Word is God is praying His Will. We are assured of an answer when we pray God's Word.

> Then said the Lord to me, You have seen well, for I am alert and active, watching over My word to perform it.
>
> Jeremiah 1:12 (AMP)

Persistence in Prayer

I sought for a man among them, that should make up the hedge, and stand in the gap before me for the land, that I should not destroy it: but I found none.

Ezekiel 22:30

God seeks men and women willing to make up the hedge; somebody willing to give himself to prayer; somebody to present the mind and will of God in the midst of situations and declare it in the natural and spirit realms.

God is looking for **Gap Standers** who will stick with prayer being confident that He will answer their prayers.

This is the confidence that we have in him, that, if we ask any thing according to his will, he heareth us: And if we know that he hear us, whatsoever we ask, we know that we have the petitions that we desired of him.

1 John 5:14-15

As an intercessor, you must have a spirit of perseverance. It really bothers me that saints rarely persevere in the way they need to. We give up too quickly and too easily. The Lord will tell us to do something, and then, if it doesn't happen like we think it should, we run with our tail between our legs and say, "Well, I guess it wasn't God's will."

Where are those who will persevere? Where are those who will stand in the face of confrontation? We must stand up with the intelligence and the boldness to make the devil back up. David called Goliath an "uncircumcised Philistine." We, too, must learn to "call it like it is." Make sure that it is God who is releasing you to say something, and then do it.

It is our responsibility to intercede; it is God's responsibility to answer and intervene in the affairs of mankind. However, when God shows you things in the Spirit as you pray for someone, remember you are not called to be their "personal Holy Ghost"! God may not allow you to share some things until sometime later — and sometimes not at all!

Pray the Word so your intercession doesn't turn into a gossip column! It's all right to talk to others who are interceding with you for purposes of clarity, but make sure you pray God's Word rather than opinions. Some intercessors do so much talking they don't pray. Make sure you are bringing glory to God.

As an intercessor, place your visions and dreams on hold. As you take the emphasis off yourself and your ministry, and keep your focus on God. He then takes care of the dreams and visions He put in your heart!

Flowing With The Vision of the Church

Every spiritual leader has a vision and a plan that God has spoken to him or her. Many times it is hindered from moving forward when the foundation is not solidly established in the spiritual realm. The intercessory prayer group needs to be wide and deep. In other words, there needs to be more than two or three persons praying for the will of God to be done in the church house.

> *Write the vision, and make it plain upon tables, that he may run that readeth it. For the vision is yet for an appointed time, but at the end it shall speak, and not lie: though it tarry, wait for it; because it will surely come, it will not tarry.*
>
> Habakkuk 2:2-3

The vision of the church must be clearly communicated so it can be backed with prayer.

Members of the congregation as well as staff should be included in intercessory prayer. Spiritual leaders must help people see that their contributions in prayer, service and finances make a tremendous difference. A greater depth of faith and loyalty will be the result.

Help members of the congregation understand the strategies of the devil. This will better help them comprehend the importance of intercession. As a pastor or someone in spiritual leadership, ask for prayer for yourself, your mate and your family.

Sometimes when a church is just getting started, the pastor fills all roles and assumes all responsibilities— he is the piano player, the praise and worship leader, the prayer leader, and (sometimes) the only prayer participant! As the church begins to grow, God will send appropriate people alongside the pastor to lead praise and worship, to lead intercession, to fill every area of the ministry of helps. Each of these people must have the vision of the pastor and must be qualified to fill the respective roles in order for the Holy Ghost to operate freely in that house.

When you go to the church house on Wednesday nights, Sunday mornings and Sunday nights (or whenever your services are held), God has something in mind. But everything He has in mind is not always accomplished, particularly if it is not backed with prayer.

Ephesians 4:16 says, **according to the effectual working in the measure of every part, maketh increase of the body unto the edifying of itself in love.** The praise and worship leader is only one part. Every person who comes alongside the pastor makes up a part of the body. Each member's function is very important, and each one must embrace the vision of the house.

When I was growing up, praise and worship were looked upon as part of the "preliminaries." Praise and worship are not preliminaries. Prayer is not a preliminary. Each of these areas plays a critical part of the whole. When done under the anointing of God, praise and worship and prayer make the pastor's job so much easier.

As a pastor or spiritual leader, have you ever felt on a Sunday morning that everything seemed to be as dead as a doornail? You try to preach a wonderful, burning word the Lord has given you, but there is no "opening"?

When I say opening, I am referring to an open heaven. Why do we want an open heaven? Because we want everything God has in mind to come down to us— salvation, deliverance, healing, signs, wonders and miracles. Let's look at this account of an "open heaven":

> *Now when all the people were baptized, it came to pass that Jesus also was baptized and while He prayed, the heaven was opened.*
>
> *And the Holy Spirit descended in bodily form like a dove upon Him, and a voice came from heaven which said, "You are My beloved Son in You I am well pleased."*
>
> Luke 3:21-22 (NKJV)

As with Jesus, when there is an open heaven, directions are given, confirmations are spoken and strategies are released. Jesus already knew He was the Son of God. This is indicated when He was in the temple at a young age confounding the leaders of that day. But God the Father knew the challenges ahead. He spoke a clear, reassuring word to Jesus before He faced the many battles of His ministry. Heaven was "open" and the glory descended.

The works of the devil are bound during intercession and during an anointed time of praise and worship.

> *Let the high praises of God be in their mouth, and a two-edged sword in their hand; To*

> *execute vengeance upon the heathen, and punishments upon the people.*
>
> Psalm 149:6, 7

When the high praises go forth in the manner as they should, they bind up the devil and his plots and schemes. In other words, the devil is all tied up!

With anointed praise and worship backed with prayer, the offering will be good and generous because the devil's stinginess is bound. With anointed praise and worship backed with prayer, there will be a free flow in the entire service. With anointed praise and worship backed with prayer, there will be an opening for the will and purpose of God to be accomplished.

The praise and worship leader must have the vision of the church and flow with it instead of flowing with his personal agenda. This is true of the intercessory prayer group as well. These areas must be aligned with God's purposes for that particular church.

Too many churches settle for people who are "talented" in the area of praise and worship but whose lifestyles are not balanced with prayer and intercession. There is no character — no fruit. If people have unclean lives, whatever comes out of them will be tainted. Their lives must be fit for God's use. They cannot be singing or praying one thing and living another.

> *Since we have the promises, dear friends, let us purify ourselves from everything that contaminates body and spirit, perfecting holiness out of reverence for God.*
>
> 2 Corinthians 7:1 (NIV)

Overcoming Discouragement

This charge I commit unto thee, son Timothy, according to the prophecies which went before on thee, that thou by them mightest war a good warfare.

1 Timothy 1:18

Intercession is war. The Word of God that is believed and spoken in prayer will oppose Satan and his agents.

One of Satan's most effective weapons against intercessors—and against all believers — is discouragement. He'll say, "Your prayers are not working." But the Word of God says **the effectual fervent prayer of a righteous man availeth much** (Jas. 5:16).

The enemy delights in making you think nothing is happening because you don't see answers to prayer manifested as quickly as you think they should. But things happen in the spirit realm when someone prays the Word. It may seem like everything in the world is trying to keep you from moving forth in God. But you can know that results will surely come to pass if you speak the Word in faith and do not negate it with your words, attitudes and actions.

One way to possess the land is through fasting and prayer. Victories are won first in the spirit realm. It is time that we get the prayer strategies of God and possess the land He has given us. After continual seasons of prayer, barriers to your answers are knocked out of the way, one by one, until the full manifestation comes. But as you begin to make headway in intercession, the devil will try to distract you through discouragement.

In a meeting we held in Philadelphia, I preached on getting back the things Satan has stolen. A young woman stood and said, "I was saved at age fifteen, and I always knew that I was to be a youth pastor. But when it didn't look like God was answering my prayer, I got discouraged. I gave up and did some things that I can't tell. My mother doesn't even know about them." She had turned from her vision because she didn't think God had answered her prayer. "But," she said, "now I know that every one of my prayers were answered. I am going to be a youth pastor." She reclaimed her purpose in God as a result of being encouraged.

People need to know that God is the same yesterday, today and forever; that He still answers prayer; that He is not slack in doing what He said in His Word. This is the day of possession of land like never before. Hook in to what God is doing in your behalf. Maybe you are facing a wall like Jericho. No one can come in and no one can go out. Whatever that wall is, if you keep on interceding, you will get through it and possess your land!

God needs intercessors. And <u>intercessors</u> need intercessors, because the enemy wants to knock them out to stop their effectiveness.

I remember when I had a miscarriage, a very trying time in my life. God raised up literally hundreds of people all around the United States to intercede for me. As a result of others "standing in the gap," I was divinely insulated from the usual period of depression and grave sense of loss. I was able to go through this trial without falling apart. I was even able to reach out to someone else and minister the Baptism of the Holy Spirit while still at home recovering. Hallelujah! I can attest to the powerful effects of intercession.

One day in my kitchen I asked the Lord, "How can we as a church better intercede for our people?" The Lord answered, "Every day you eat at least three times." He was showing me that I was going to church three times a week and sometimes more often. In order to better intercede for the people, pray for the leader of the church every time you eat your physical food. Prayer <u>does</u> make a difference.

As a pastor or spiritual leader, let your people know how much you need their prayers and how much you appreciate and value them as persons. This will cause church members to bond together, and, at the same time, strengthen a sense of acceptance and belonging.

Your "Shunammite Blessing" Is In The House

For as the heavens are higher than the earth, so are my ways higher than your ways, and my thoughts than your thoughts.

Isaiah 55:9

Although God's ways and thoughts are higher than ours, Scripture does not say we can't know His thoughts and His ways. In intercession, we can move up to His level. It is in the presence of God that we learn His thoughts and His ways and begin the process of becoming like Him.

God has something in mind when He calls a man or a woman to minister. He will hook you up with certain people and bring the Holy Ghost, the One called alongside, to help, aid, advise and counsel. When God calls us, He has something in mind. It is a cause. He has you situated right where you are because there is a cause in that place that He wants you to help carry out.

My husband and I are part of a team called alongside Bishop Carlton Pearson to carry out a God-ordained cause. The first year we were with Pastor Carlton, my husband Tomm worked an entire year without receiving a dime even though he worked circles around many of the people who were being paid.

Back then I had more problems with my flesh than I do now, so I used to get angry and frustrated. I didn't realize that Tommy was setting us up for a blessing.

> *One day Elisha went to Shunem. And a well-to-do woman was there, who urged him to stay for a meal. So whenever he came by, he stopped there to eat. She said to her husband, "I know that this man who often comes our way is a holy man of God. Let's make a small room on the roof and put in it a bed and a table, a chair and a lamp for him. Then he can stay there whenever he comes to us."*
>
> *One day when Elisha came, he went up to his room and lay down there. He said to his servant Gehazi, "Call the Shunammite." So he called her, and she stood before him. Elisha said to him, "Tell her, 'You have gone*

to all this trouble for us. Now what can be done for you? Can we speak on your behalf to the king or the commander of the army?'"

She replied, "I have a home among my own people."

"What can be done for her?" Elisha asked.

Gehazi said, "Well, she has no son and her husband is old."

Then Elisha said, "Call her." So he called her, and she stood in the doorway.

"About this time next year," Elisha said, "you will hold a son in your arms."

"No, my lord," she objected. "Don't mislead your servant, O man of God!"

But the woman became pregnant, and the next year about that same time she gave birth to a son, just as Elisha had told her.

2 Kings 4:8-17 (NIV)

The Shunammite woman saw a need and was willing to fulfill it with no strings attached. At her own expense she took the weight off of God's servant by "coming alongside to help." As a result of her sensitivity, God gave her an unexpected blessing in her area of need which was barrenness.

While my husband was busy setting us up for a blessing, I was pouting! I'm so thankful that God didn't pay any attention to that! We are called alongside to help in whatever capacity is needed.

As a spiritual leader, if you have not been getting the people you need to help you carry out the cause, first ask the Lord. "Am I in the right place?" If you are, then ask how you need to push through in prayer so these people will manifest.

Whether you are a pastor, a traveling minister, or in the ministry of helps, you need people to come alongside to help you. When you are the one working alongside, sometimes you feel like saying , "God, I'm ready for my own ministry." But are you ready to minister wherever God puts you? Cleaning bathrooms? Changing diapers? Are you ready to do whatever it takes for the will of God to be done?

My husband and I are now itinerant ministers. We are faithful in the house where God called us, and Higher Dimensions Family Church is still our home base. As we go out to minister, our pastor sends us with his blessings —and, I might add, a highly favorable written recommendation! When God is moving you into your own ministry, He will move you spiritually from level to level and from glory to glory.

- 11 -

Changing "Barren" Circumstances Through Intercession

In First Samuel, chapter 1, we learn that Samuel was conceived as a result of the intercession of his mother, Hannah. This was not a small thing: Hannah was a barren woman. Sometimes in intercession it may seem that what you are doing has no life to it. Nothing seems to be going on. You feel barren.

Hannah's husband Elkanah had another wife whose name was Peninnah. Hannah means "gracious," while Peninnah means "a pearl." Unfortunately Peninnah didn't act like a pearl! Peninnah had children by Elkanah, but Hannah was barren. So Peninnah treated Hannah with great disrespect every day. "She messed with her!"

Once a year, Elkanah, his wives, and his children by Peninnah would go to the House of the Lord taking gifts for Eli the priest. At these times the other women always belittled Hannah for her barrenness.

Hannah hurt because she wanted a child, and it didn't seem that she was being noticed. Hannah was messed with so badly that the Bible says it caused her "bitterness of soul" (v.10).

Each of us has an enemy of our soul who comes to mess with us. This enemy says, "Look how long you have been here in your so-called ministry. Now look at what is happening to so-and-so. They are getting breakthroughs, and you're not doing anything!"

When you see someone else moving ahead in his or her ministry while you seem to be sitting on the backside of the desert, don't allow bitterness and jealousy to come. God is working on you.

Notice these words in verse 9: so **Hannah rose up.** After being talked about and messed with year after year, Hannah decided that she was going to get up. Hannah did something: she rose up.

The enemy has attacked some of us until we have laid down our gifts. We have stopped functioning the way God has called and ordained us to function. It is time to rise up. God is calling us to come up higher — to do something to change the barrenness in our lives. God does not want us to bring Him down to where we are. He wants us to come up to where He is.

> *So Hannah rose up after they had eaten in Shiloh, and after they had drunk. Now Eli the priest sat upon a seat by a post of the temple of the Lord.*
>
> *And she was in bitterness of soul, and prayed unto the Lord, and wept sore.*
>
> *And she vowed a vow, and said, O Lord of hosts, if thou wilt indeed look on the affliction of thine handmaid, and remember me... (v. 9-11).*

This is your time to be remembered. You have talked about it with your friends, and you have cried about it. But now it is time to go to God and say, "Remember me."

Someone said, "It may be your turn, but it may not be your time." But for some, it's your turn <u>and</u> it's your time! It's time to come forth in the will and purpose of God. It's time to get up. Say, "I will arise. I will get up. Yes, I will!"

> *Remember me, and not forget thine handmaid, but wilt give unto thine handmaid a man child, then I will give him unto the Lord all the days of*

> *his life, and there shall no razor come upon his head (v. 11).*

Hannah made a vow. She had been waiting her turn.

> *And it came to pass, as she continued praying before the Lord ... (v. 12).*

Hannah continued to pray. Some of us have given up too easily in our praying. If it doesn't happen tomorrow or next year (or two or three years from now), we start giving up. The Bible says that Hannah continued to pray. Year after year she experienced the problems. She was prodded by her enemy and she cried. Wipe away your tears! It's time to rise up. It's time to push forth into the will and purpose of God.

> *And it came to pass, as she continued praying before the Lord, that Eli marked her mouth.*
>
> *Now Hannah, she spake in her heart; only her lips moved, but her voice was not heard: therefore Eli thought she had been drunken (vv. 12, 13).*

Have you ever prayed about something to the point where all you could do was cry? The tears roll down your face, and there are no more words. You've been praying for change. Change in your house.

Change in your church. And sometimes nothing comes out; only your mouth is moving. Have you prayed to that point? Jesus prayed to the point where His sweat was as drops of blood.

Eli thought Hannah was drunk.

> *And Eli said unto her, How long wilt thou be drunken? put away thy wine from thee.*
>
> *And Hannah answered and said, No, my lord, I am a woman of a sorrowful spirit: I have drunk neither wine nor strong drink, but have poured out my soul before the Lord (vv. 14, 15).*

God wants us to pour out our soul. The devil tries to capitalize most on our emotions. So what are we to do? We are to pour out our soul. We are to pour out our emotions. We are to pour out our hurts. We are to pour out all the things that have been hurting us in order for the Lord to fill us afresh. God says, "Pour out your soul."

If we are not alert the enemy will keep us down by hitting us in the soul realm. But Hannah poured out her soul. We intercede when we get out of the soul realm into the spirit realm.

Hannah answered Eli:

> *Count not thine handmaid for a daughter of Belial: for out of the abundance of my complaint and grief have I spoken hitherto (v. 16).*

Many of us are not up front and honest with God. We need to be. God is not going to slap us because we are honest with Him. God knows our thoughts, He knows our uprising, He knows our downsitting (Ps. 139). He knows everything about us anyway. So we might as well tell Him the truth.

> *Then Eli answered and said, Go in peace: and the God of Israel grant thee thy petition that thou hast asked of him (v. 17).*

It is best for us just to be "raw honest" with God. He already knows what we are dealing with. Tell Him what is hurting you. Don't talk to everybody else about it. Let it be between you and God. Pour out your soul to Him. Deal with the thing that is messing with you.

After Hannah rose up and poured out her soul; after she dealt with her will, her intellect and her emotions; after she got "raw honest" with God; after she talked with the man of God and said, "No, I am not drunk as you suppose;" then God could grant her petition.

And she said, Let thine handmaid find grace in thy sight. So the woman went her way, and did eat, and her countenance was no more sad (v. 18).

Once you know that the Lord has heard your prayer, then you will no longer operate out of your soul. You will not be swayed by other people. Someone can say you'll never be a preacher or you'll never be a teacher. But there is something on the inside of you that says, "I know that I know that I am called of God, and it does not matter what anyone says. It is so, in Jesus' name." Why? Because it was settled in intercession.

What is wrong with us today? We don't settle enough things in intercession. We don't stay in intercession long enough to take our souls captive. We don't stay in intercession long enough to take our emotions captive. We don't settle it. You've got to get it settled in your soul. Then you can go to God, and He will say, "It's all right." No more fasting. No more crying.

When you have settled things in prayer you can ignore the devil and just go on about your business. The Bible says Hannah had been so hurt, she couldn't even eat. But after Hannah settled things in her spirit, Peninnah could say whatever she wanted to say. Hannah would just smile and say, "Give me one of those chicken legs and some more of those mustard greens. I need a few yams on the side. Give me some cornbread and potatoes."

The people said, "My God, what's wrong with this woman? Before she wouldn't even eat, now, she's eating us out of house and home!"

It was because Hannah had received her answer. How did she get her answer? She hung in there. She had a "knowing."

When you get a knowing, it's like you have the "eye of a tiger." You focus only on what God is saying to you. Nothing can stop you, nothing can pull you back. God is still the One Who hears and answers prayer. But you must hang in there in prayer.

We've got to get beyond what I call the "Touch, Lord" prayer or the "Touch, Lord" ministry. A minister prays right before the service, "Touch the people, Lord." God has entrusted lives into his hands, and, instead of being diligent in prayer, he says, "Touch, Lord." He hasn't been before God, yet he is getting ready to handle God's people. Lord, deliver us from the "Touch, Lord" mentality!

This is a problem with many saints today. We want to pray quick prayers, but we don't want to hang in there. I'm telling you, Jesus is our perfect example. He hung on in prayer.

The Bible tells us Jesus was up praying way before morning. He was persistent to pray because thousands were waiting on Him for their healing and deliverance. If Jesus, the very Son of God, had to pray, what about you and me? We've got to hang on in prayer.

Hannah knew that God had heard her. The man of God had spoken and said it was going to be all right now. **Go in peace** (said Eli) **and the God of Israel grant thee thy petition** (1 Sam.1:17).

Once you have settled things in your soul, the devil's old ways won't work anymore. Hannah had worked it out of her soul. So when Peninnah said, "Look at my children," Hannah just walked on because she knew she was going to have a child. She knew that God's promised child was on the way.

> *And they rose up in the morning early, and worshipped before the Lord, and returned (v.19).*

I imagine that Hannah's worship was different this time because she knew that she knew her prayers were heard. She... *worshipped before the Lord, and returned, and came to their house to Ramah: and Elkanah knew Hannah his wife* (there was intimacy between Hannah and her husband); *and the Lord remembered her (v. 19).*

We, too, must know God. We can know Him by spending time in His presence in the Word and in prayer. Ministry and life spring out of an intimate relationship with the Lord. Whatever we do should be birthed out of time spent in prayer with God.

We can be so busy with the work of the Lord that we forget God Himself. Our strength should come from Him rather than from the flesh. We are created to walk in the Spirit and not fulfill the lust of the flesh. The flesh always lusts. It always wants approval. It always wants a pat on the back. If you don't get your pat on the back in your private time, you will not get it in public.

Let your pat be, "Good and faithful servant, I am going to make you a ruler over many things. I am going to do some things for you because you have been faithful."

The Lord remembered Hannah. He remembered what He had promised her.

> *Wherefore it came to pass, when the time was come about after Hannah had conceived, that she bare a son, and called his name Samuel, saying, Because I have asked him of the Lord.*

And the man Elkanah, and all his house, went up to offer unto the Lord the yearly sacrifice, and his vow.

> But Hannah went not up; for she said unto her husband, I will not go up until the child be weaned, and then I will bring him, that he may appear before the Lord, and there abide for ever.
>
> (1 Samuel 1:20-22)

For how long? Forever! Hannah interceded for Samuel that he would go before God and remain there forever. Why do you think that Samuel could hear from God? This woman— his mother — had poured out her soul for him.

If you have children and you haven't interceded for them, it is not too late with God. He still can move and touch and work on behalf of your children. Pour out your soul before the Lord. If your children have been acting crazy, acting as though they didn't belong to God or you, pour out your soul unto the Lord.

> And Elkanah her husband said unto her, Do what seemeth thee good; tarry until thou have weaned him; only the Lord establish his word. So the woman abode, and gave her son suck until she weaned him.

And when she had weaned him, she took him up with her (vv. 23, 24).

Hannah had vowed to God that her son would be returned to Him and he would worship Him all the days of his life. She made a vow and she kept her word.

Maybe you have been on the backside of the desert, wondering what is going on. You have been making a lot of vows. Are you going to keep your word? When God needs you to do something, or go somewhere, will you still keep your vow?

> *When thou vowest a vow unto God, defer not to pay it; for he hath no pleasure in fools: pay that which thou hast vowed.*
>
> *Better is it that thou shouldest not vow, than that thou shouldest vow and not pay.*
>
> Ecclesiastes 5:4, 5

Hannah kept her vow to the Lord.

> *And when she had weaned him, she took him up with her, with three bullocks, and one ephah of flour, and a bottle of wine, and brought him unto the house of the Lord in Shiloh: and the child was young.*

And they slew a bullock, and brought the child to Eli.

And she said, O my lord, as thy soul liveth, my lord, I am the woman that stood by thee here, praying unto the Lord.

For this child I prayed; and the Lord hath given me my petition which I asked of him:

Therefore also I have lent him to the Lord; as long as he liveth he shall be lent to the Lord. And he worshipped the Lord there.

(1 Samuel 1:24-28)

Let me tell you something about this boy Samuel who was called of the Lord. He had a mother who prayed. I don't think she really knew that she was birthing a man who would be a prophet to the nations.

What are you birthing? Who are you standing in the gap for? Yes, we stand in the gap on behalf of our own ministries, but what about other ministries or people you have been called alongside to help? Are you willing to give of yourself until God births what He has in mind for them?

My husband and I still fast, pray and undergird our pastor of more than sixteen years. Why? Because we want the will of God to be done in the earth. It is not about a man, it is about a cause. Don't try to do what the leader of a ministry is called to do. God is saying, "Get under their calling. Undergird them in prayer."

Your blessing, even your future, is in the house where God has placed you. Do whatever it takes for the vision of that house to come to full fruition.

You see, it was in the House of the Lord that I learned to pray. It was in that house that sensitivity came. It was in that house that I learned how to serve.

It was in the House of the Lord where Hannah received the word that she would have a son. She was not told within the confines of her own house that a man-child was going to come to her. What if she hadn't gone up to the House of the Lord, but just stayed at home?

Some of us get hurt and we want to stay at home or sit in the back seat at church and pout. That's when the enemy can cause things to fester on the inside of us. But it's time to push through the barrenness in our lives in prayer and come up to a higher place with God.

Jesus — The Greatest Intercessor

Jesus understands intercession because He is the Greatest Intercessor who has ever been, Who now is, and Who ever will be.

Wherefore he is able also to save them to the uttermost that come unto God by him, seeing he ever liveth to make intercession for them.

Hebrews 7:25

Technically the term <u>intercession</u> describes approaching a king to present one's petition as Queen Esther did on behalf of her people Israel. An intercessor endeavors to repair the gap or breach between God and mankind — by standing in the gap. Intercessors link the mind and will of God to man's need.

Intercession is spiritual warfare, and the responsibility is two- fold. The intercessor not only gets in the gap, but also <u>remains</u> in the gap petitioning the Lord until the "hedge" (or wall of protection and prevention) has been built.

Jesus lives to make intercession for you and me. Jesus meets with God to entreat Him or to converse with Him concerning us. He is enthusiastic about seeking God on our behalf. You can be assured that you are covered in intercession by the Greatest Intercessor!

Sometimes I vividly picture Jesus at the right hand of the Father. When the devil, that old accuser of the brethren, tries to mess with God's people, I see Jesus tapping the Father on the shoulder in our defense. Doesn't that make you feel good to know that Jesus is constantly tapping God the Father's shoulder on our behalf? This is demonstrated in Luke 22:31-32 (NKJ):

> *And the Lord said, "Simon, Simon! Indeed, Satan has asked for you, that he may sift you as wheat.*
>
> *"But I have prayed (interceded) for you, that your faith should not fail; and when you have returned to Me, strengthen your brethren."*

Jesus declared to Peter that Satan desired to confuse him and decrease his faith to a point of inactivity. But Jesus, by way of intercession, had been standing in Peter's defense. Jesus made Peter aware that He had personally toiled in intercession for him to ensure that Satan's plan would not happen. Jesus arrested the attack of the enemy in the supernatural first. Jesus also instructed Peter that when he was strong again, he was to become an intercessor for others. He was to become a **Gap Stander,** a repairer of breaches.

I am sure that many pastors, spiritual leaders and other believers feel as if they have gone through a sifting — a time of confusion, trials and wavering. That's because the devil desires to destroy God's ultimate plan for your life. But Jesus is interceding on your behalf. When the gap is filled, when the wall has been built for you, it is then your responsibility to become a **Gap Stander** and build walls for others. Thus the body of Christ will become a fortified, united front standing against the enemy.

Jesus, our example in intercession, stood in the gap. Indeed, He is even yet standing in the gap for us.

G.A.P. is my acronym for "**G**od **A**nswers **P**rayer." And S.T.A.N.D.E.R means "**S**ticking **T**ogether **A**nd **N**ot **D**oubting **E**ternal **R**equests."
Stick to it! Persevere in intercession. The things God has declared **will** be granted.

> *Now this is the confidence that we have Him, that if we ask anything according to His will, He hears us.*

> *And if we know that He hears us, whatever we ask we know that we have the petitions that we have asked of Him.*
>
> 1 John 5:14-15 (NKJV)

Despite any resistance you can be confident that God will perform His will. But we must ask according to His will. We must intercede with tenacity on a consistent basis. The problem with many of us is that we don't intercede until something happens.

> *The earnest (heartfelt, continued) prayer of a righteous man makes tremendous power available [dynamic in its working].*
>
> James 5:16 (AMP)

Persevere until you reach a point of victory in the spirit. Our intercession makes tremendous power available to ensure victory. Once victory is achieved in the spirit realm, it will manifest in the natural realm.
Jesus cried out from the cross **Father, forgive them, for they know not what they do** (Lk. 23:34). This is another example of Jesus as a **Gap Stander.** Although Jesus tasted death for us, He never vacated his position in intercession. He stood in the gap, enduring the cross and despising the shame for

the joy that was set before Him (Heb. 12:2). We are that joy that was set before Him.

When we face situations and circumstances, God wants us to stand until something happens on the inside of us, until our perception of our circumstances are altered in His presence. Jesus persevered in prayer until He said, **Not my will, but thine be done.** We, too, must learn to pray that way.

God wants us to remember that Jesus is interceding for us. When we know that God is doing something on our behalf, it expands our level of confidence. The Bible instructs us **to come boldly unto the throne of grace, that we may obtain mercy, and find grace to help in time of need** (Heb. 4:16).

The problem is, we have not realized our position in God. As intercessors — as **Gap Standers** — we have authority from God. We have been raised up and seated <u>together</u> with Jesus in heavenly places (Eph. 2:6). From God's perspective, we are there with Him right now.

Many of us have been praying from an "earth level." You can't really see much from a natural perspective. It is as though a forest surrounds you and all you can see are the trees. All we see are the negative situations and circumstances. But when you start interceding "with God's heart," — from His level — you will be like an eagle! You will have a heavenly perspective, and you will not just see the problems.

You must first go into God's presence — go to the holy ground — to obtain His heart and mind. Then go back to the battleground, go back into the adverse circumstances, with the Lord's overcoming strategies.

> *But they that wait upon the Lord shall renew their strength; they shall mount up with wings as eagles; they shall run, and not be weary; and they shall walk, and not faint.*
>
> Isaiah 40:31

To **wait upon the Lord** means "to be intertwined with."[5] This represents an intimate relationship. God is saying that we need to get wrapped up, tied up, and tangled up in Him. An intercessor must have a close relationship with God before he or she can become effective in petitioning the Lord on behalf of the church or anyone else. In our travels in ministry, we find many people who are faithful in church attendance and in filling their posts. But their relationship with the One for whom they work could stand some improvement.

Others have become weary in their posts because they have not taken the time to be refreshed in the Lord. Acts 3:19 says **the times of refreshing shall**

come from the presence of the Lord. We've got to turn this thing around. Let's not go into the 21st Century with tired, weary and unprepared spirits. We must be prepared to move forward with greater fervor in the Lord than ever before — especially in the area of intercession.

---
5 Miriam Webster Dictionary INC., (Springdale, Massachusetts, U.S.A., 1983).